THE INDISPENSABLE ROLE OF THE HOLY SPIRIT

BY DR. BILL BENNETT

The Indispensable Role of The Holy Spirit

Copyright © 2010

ISBN-13: 978-1-935256-07-6

Published by L'Edge Press

A ministry of Upside Down Ministries, Inc.

PO Box 2567

Boone, NC 28607

For information on Mentoring Men for the Master, please visit our web site at www.MentoringMen.net

Man has two great needs – Pardon and Power. God met our need for pardon at Calvary, and He met our need for power at Pentecost. Humankind must have these two great gifts, the gift of Pardon, and the gift of Power, the Holy Spirit, in order to live in the fullness of the gospel and impact their world with its redeeming message. However, for 2000 years man has tended to recognize his need for pardon, but has overlooked his great need for power. In fact the Holy Spirit has become "The Forgotten God" in most evangelical churches, resulting in an anemic, joyless, powerless church. It is for this reason that I have written this book. I do not feel qualified to address such an infinitely deep and mysterious subject. But I believe the Holy Spirit has led me to do so. So I earnestly pray that what I say from the pages of the Bible, supported by a few personal experiences, may cause the readers to embrace and experience the wonderful, life-transforming power of the mighty third person of the Holy Trinity – the Forgotten God, the Holy Spirit.

Dr. Bill Bennett

Founder President

Mentoring Men for the Master, Int

Table Of Contents

Foreword

I have not written this book as a "know it all" about pneumatology or the mysterious doctrine of the Holy Spirit, but as one who has searched the Scriptures concerning the Holy Spirit for fifty years, read extensively on the subject, and experienced His redeeming and liberating power in my own life, and am still seeking to know and experience more of his inexhaustible blessings in my life. While I realize that I have only scratched the surface of the subject, I am convinced of the "Indispensable Role of the Holy Spirit" in every aspect of Christian theology and Christian experience. And whatever your view may be, I pray that you will prayerfully read, with an open heart, the overwhelming evidence in the Scriptures of His "Indispensable Role" in every aspect of Christianity, including your salvation, sanctification, your devotion to Jesus Christ, your grasp of the Bible, your ability to crucify the flesh, your understanding of the life of Jesus, and your quest for the abundant life. Having done this, provided you are indwelt by the Holy Spirit through the new birth, I am confident that the Holy Spirit Himself will testify to you of your desperate need of His power in your life and lead you to surrender to Him on a daily basis, if you have not already done so.

Thank you.

The Indispensable Role Of The Holy Spirit
Who Is The Holy Spirit?

"The Holy Spirit leaves no footprints in the sand." These words are from Abraham Kuper's classic work on the Holy Spirit. In contrast Jesus did leave footprints in the sand. He was God incarnate and dwelt or tabernacled among men (John 1:14) for thirty three years. His disciples walked with Him for three and one half years, they saw Him with their eyes, they even handled Him with their hands (1 John 1:1-3) and watched "the sand spilling over His feet as He trod the shores of the Sea of Galilee."[1] But the Holy Spirit is like the wind. "The wind blows where it wishes, and you hear the sound of it, but cannot tell where it comes from and where it is going" (John 3:8). These are the very words of Jesus used to describe the Holy Spirit to Nicodemus. The Holy Spirit is mysterious and unpredictable but none the less real. We cannot explain Him, but like the wind we can experience His Power, which is more ferocious than the wind.

---

[1] R. C. Sproul, *The Mystery of the Holy Spirit*, p. 7.

Moreover, we know and accept by faith what the Holy Scriptures reveal about the mysterious Third Person of the Trinity. So please note seven basic truths about Him:

1. The Holy Spirit is a Person. Jesus is careful never to call Him an "It" (an abstract force or power) but He always refers to Him as a Person (John 15:26; 16:13). The Holy Spirit identifies Himself as a Person. "...the Holy Spirit said, now separate to Me Barnabas and Saul for the work to which I have called them (Acts 13:2). Note the two personal pronouns, "Me," and "I." The Holy Spirit performs personal tasks. He teaches us (John 14:26), He comforts us (John 14:16). He leads us (Romans 8:14), He prays for us (Romans 8:26). Furthermore, He possesses all the traits of human personality: emotion, will, mind (Ephesians 4:30; 1 Cor. 12:11; Romans 8:27).

2. The Holy Spirit is a Divine Person. He is nowhere absent and everywhere present. He is Omniscient; He knows all things (1 Cor. 2:10-11). He is also Omnipresent – He is present everywhere (Psalm 139:7-8). He is also Omnipotent or all powerful. He does the kind of works only God can perform as

seen in the work of creation (Genesis 1:1-2) and redemption (Hebrews 9:14).

3. The Holy Spirit indwells every true believer (Romans 8:9a), and He desires a personal relationship with every believer (James 4:5).

4. The Holy Spirit is the Great Remembrancer, reminding and teaching us of all the teachings of Jesus (John 14:26).

5. The Holy Spirit is the Revealer of Jesus Christ and the Reproducer of His life and power in the life of the believer (John 16:13-14).

6. The Holy Spirit is God. The apostle Peter accused Ananias of lying to the Holy Spirit (Acts 5:3) and in the next verse says "Thou hast not lied unto men, but unto God" (Acts 5:4).

7. He who does not know God the Holy Spirit does not know God at all. The apostle Paul asserts that "no man can say that Jesus is Lord but by the Holy Spirit" (1 Cor. 12:3b). J. B. Phillips expresses this truth in astounding words, "Every time we say, 'I believe in the Holy Spirit,' we mean that we believe that there is a living God able and willing to enter human personality and change it."[2]

Thus the Holy Spirit is indispensable in the life of Jesus, the life of every believer, in Christian theology, and every important fact related to true Christianity. I have written the following chapters of this book to prove this fact.

In my first pastorate out of the seminary, a faithful member of my flock asked me this question, "Pastor, do Baptists believe in the Holy Spirit?" To which I responded, "Jay, why would you ask me this question?" He replied, "Well, I am a fireman and work with a guy who is a Pentecostal and he is always talking about the Holy Spirit, but we almost never mention the Holy Spirit in our church, so I was wondering if the Holy Spirit was for Pentecostals but not us Baptists."

---

[2] Ibid. p. 0

In response to Jay's question, we would tend to brush it aside and say, "Well, it is a pity Jay is so ignorant." But there is something far more serious reflected in his question, namely, many conservative Bible believing church members know practically nothing about the Person and work of the Holy Spirit. In fact I suspect many are like Jay and believe the Holy Spirit is for Pentecostals or some "lunatic fringe" group, and we should leave the Holy Spirit to them and not be concerned about the "strange doctrine" of the Holy Spirit. Example: As a young pastor I discovered there was much emphasis on the Holy Spirit in the life of the early church, as stated in the Book of Acts. Therefore, I asked an older respected pastor and my mentor if he did not think that Baptists should give more attention to the Holy Spirit, to which he replied, "Well Bill, you should not be concerned about the Holy Spirit. All we need is Jesus, so let's just stick to Him," as if to indicate there is no relationship of Jesus to the Holy Spirit, when the Bible clearly states that it is by the ministry of the Holy Spirit that we know and experience Jesus in our hearts. Another brother and fellow pastor politely pleaded with me to "go easy" on the Holy Spirit in my preaching, declaring to me, "Bill, with your ability to preach and expound Scripture, you would become a major leader among Southern Baptists if you would say less about the Holy Spirit," clearly meaning that unless I did abandon my emphasis on the Holy Spirit that the "brethren"

5

would distrust me to be a "Charismatic" and not trust me in places of high leadership.

As the "brethren" were telling me not to lay any emphasis on the Holy Spirit, other brothers were decrying the fact of our great spiritual need. Example: Dr. R. G. Lee, the legendary Southern Baptist preacher and my neighbor and mentor for years, said in my hearing these words, "The average service in a Southern Baptist church at 11 AM is so cold that you could skate down the aisles on the ice." A former president of the SBC and Professor of Preaching at Louisville Seminary, Dr. Carl Bates, made this remark to me in 1974, "Bill, if the Holy Spirit were suddenly withdrawn from the average Southern Baptist church, they would go on operating as usual and would not even know anything had happened." As to my own experience, a very few persons in my churches would at times go to extremes and appear to be on the verge of fanaticism and two or three people would express this fear to me, to which I replied, "I will make a deal with you: I will "cool off" the "fanatics" if you will heat up the corpses.

In light of the many views of the Holy Spirit, I think it might be helpful to spell out ten attitudes concerning the Holy Spirit which I have encountered in my ministry:

1. Persons who pay lip service to the Holy Spirit in the Doxology and then never think of Him thereafter.

2. Persons who virtually worship the Holy Spirit and His gifts. David Wilkerson, the renown charismatic leader, has charged some charismatics with making Pentecost a Christ-less event, focusing entirely on the Holy Spirit, when it is totally Christo-centric, Christ Himself having sent the Holy Spirit as His first act after His exaltation (Acts 2:33).

3. An earnest and relatively small group who believe that the Holy Spirit leads them into the "handling of snakes," the "drinking of poison," and even "the raising of the dead." Example: A faithful member of my church in Houston, Texas, died. The next day a faithful member of the same flock came to my study, requesting that I go with him to the funeral home and "raise" this lady from the dead. I tried to reason with this guy as to his

error, but he left charging me with unbelief and I never laid eyes on him again.

4. Those who believe that Pentecost is a denomination, as I have explained above, and if not a Pentecostal, the Holy Spirit is not for them.

5. Several groups who baptize only in the name of Jesus, as if the Father and the Holy Spirit had no part in personal salvation. Example: A member of this group began to visit the church I was pastoring and liked our church so much he desired to move his membership to our church. Therefore, he asked that I baptize him but only in the name of Jesus. I tried to show him from the Bible that God the Father (Ephesians 1:1-6), God the Son (Ephesians 1:7-8) and God the Holy Spirit (Ephesians 1:33ff) played an indispensable role in his salvation, but he refused to believe, whereupon I said to him, "I cannot baptize you only in the Name of Jesus. That would be blasphemy in my judgment."

6. A large group who believe the work of the Holy Spirit begins and ends with the new birth, and all true believers are already filled with the Holy Spirit. It is certainly true that when one is born again He receives all the Holy Spirit as a Person. However, the Bible plainly commands such persons to be "continually filled" or controlled by the Holy Spirit, and also to "walk continually in the Holy Spirit" (Ephesians 5:18; Galatians 5:16). Thus you get all the Holy Spirit in the new birth, but the Holy Spirit does not get all of you. In reality, all our blessings in Christ are conveyed to the believer through the Holy Spirit which occurs throughout the life of every Christian. God's great and final word to the church opens with this astounding promise in Ephesians 1:3, "Blessed be the God and Father of our Lord Jesus Christ who blessed us with every spiritual blessing – the pneumtike – brought by the Holy Spirit – in Christ Jesus."

7. Most Pentecostals and some Charismatics, but not all, insist that the proof of being filled with the Holy Spirit is speaking in tongues, though Paul plainly teaches that not everyone, even in apostolic time, spoke in tongues (1 Cor. 12:30b). Example: One of the most valuable persons I ever had on my staff lived many years thinking he was a "second rate" Christian, if one at

9

all, because he did not speak in tongues. Then he saw the error of what he had been taught and became a joyous, victorious believer and served as media director of a large Southern Baptist church I pastored.

8. Some teach that the baptism of the Holy Spirit is a second work of grace, the evidence of which is the eradication of one's sinful nature, not the speaking in tongues. The Bible never speaks of a "second work" of grace in this way. I prefer calling the "infilling" of the Holy Spirit the last half of the first work; for the same Holy Spirit who enters one's life in the new birth is the same Holy Spirit who desires to fill us continually (Ephesians 5:18).

9. Those who believe and testify to the experience of "rivers of living waters literally welling up in their stomach," resulting in power to heal and to do other miracles. Example: The most visible Pentecostal on the modern scene described his experience to me in these terms: "God has used you greatly already, but if you would have this experience of living waters welling up in your soul, you would change the world," and then added, "You are a Jesus man," implying I was not a "Holy Spirit man," but

to which I replied, "Indeed, I am a Jesus man, but also a Holy Spirit man. I don't believe you can have one without the other."

10. Finally, there are those, who adhering to the Scriptures in my opinion, regard the Holy Spirit as the "Executive" in the God-Head, always speaking and exalting Jesus, and making real in human experience all that Jesus purchased in His death, burial and resurrection, first convicting people of their lostness in sin and need of the Savior, then giving the new birth to them who will repent and trust Jesus, entering into the converted to indwell them forever, and finally controlling them (infilling) continually as they surrender to Him daily. Note: an "executive" is one who carries out the purpose of another. The divine Executive, the Holy Spirit, has come to indwell every believer. The purpose of His indwelling is to "execute" or to do in us all that the Savior has come to do for us. Christ made salvation available, and the Holy Spirit makes it effective. Christ bought redemption; the Holy Spirit brought redemption, without which redemption would only be a conception in the head but not a saving experience in the heart.

In light of these varying views, it must be obvious to anyone that there is a desperate need for God's people to know the importance of the indispensable role of the Holy Spirit in the Christian life. How can we know this? I have wrestled with this question for fifty years and I have come to this conclusion: We need to realize the blessings we would miss and be without if the Holy Spirit had not come or if He did not even exist. I will, therefore, list these blessings below.

As I have searched the Scriptures, I have found an "amazing series of CAN'TS" relating to His touch in the lives of God's children:

You cannot be saved without the Holy Spirit (John 3:3-7).

You cannot know you are saved without the Holy Spirit (Romans 8:16).

You cannot understand the Bible without the Holy Spirit (1 Cor. 2:14).

You cannot pray without the Holy Spirit (Ephesians 6:18; Jude 1:20).

You cannot have a Christ-like life without the Holy Spirit (Galatians 5:22-23).

You cannot worship without the Holy Spirit (John 4:24; Phil. 3:3).

You cannot witness without the Holy Spirit (Acts 1:8).

You have no spiritual gifts or spiritual giftedness without the Holy Spirit (Romans 12:6-8; 1 Cor. 12:4, 11, 27-31).

You cannot serve God without the Holy Spirit (1 Cor. 12:7).

You cannot overcome sin or the flesh in your life without the Holy Spirit (Romans 8:13; Gal. 5:11).

You cannot preach or teach with any effectiveness without the Holy Spirit (1 Cor. 2:4-5; 1 Thess. 1:5).

You cannot bubble up with hope without the Holy Spirit (Romans 15:13).

In the words of David Jeremiah, "Without the Holy Spirit, we have nothing."[3]

[3] David Jeremiah, *God in You*, p. 26.

I. The Indispensable Role of the Holy Spirit
In the Life of Jesus

The gospel writers never mention any of Jesus' physical attributes, nor do they speak at all about his human talents or abilities. Instead they write about the power of the Holy Spirit and wisdom displayed in His life. "When Jesus took on human flesh, He chose to live under the limitations that come with a physical body. That doesn't mean He ceased to be divine, but He willingly set aside His rights as God and lived as a human. And being limited by His physical condition, He was forced to rely upon the Holy Spirit as His source of wisdom and power."[4]

We see the presence of the Holy Spirit in Jesus' life in a clear and visible way in the following episodes of His life.

---

[4] Henry and Melvin Blackaby, *Experiencing the Spirit*, Colorado Springs, Col.: Multonomah Publishing, 2009, p. 47.

1. The Virgin Birth – Jesus Christ was conceived in the womb of Mary by the power of the Holy Spirit. Both Matthew and Luke make it abundantly clear that Jesus was born of the virgin Mary through the supernatural power of the Holy Spirit. Matthew 1:18 declares that Mary "was found with child of the Holy Spirit." In Matthew 1:20, the angel said to Joseph, "that which is conceived in her is of the Holy Spirit." In other words, Jesus became man, the Son of man, through the miraculous work of the Holy Spirit. There could have been no real incarnation without the supernatural activity of the Holy Spirit.

Now what parallel to this do we find in the life of the believer? Just as the Holy Spirit planted an incorruptible seed of life in Mary which resulted in the birth of Jesus, the God-Man, so the Holy Spirit takes the incorruptible seed of the Word of God, implants it into the soul of a believing person, which makes him a new creation, a child of God (1 Peter 1:23).

The new birth is no more possible without the Holy Spirit than was the virgin birth of Jesus. You can no more become a Son of God without the Holy Spirit than Jesus could have become the Son of Man without Him. His earthly life began through the work of the Holy Spirit. Your life with God begins through His regenerating work.

2. Jesus was anointed for His public ministry by the power of the Holy Spirit. Jesus was now thirty years old. He had lived a perfect, sinless life. He had never had an impure thought. He had never grieved the Father. He had attended the synagogue. He was as holy as was God the Father in heaven. Yet Jesus had never preached a sermon, never worked a miracle, never won a soul – all this waited until Jesus was anointed with the Holy Spirit at His baptism (Acts 10:38). Maynard James points out, "That the incarnate Son of God should need to be filled with the Holy Spirit is a great mystery; but it has unmistakable significance for all Christians today. We do not read of a single miracle being performed by the sinless Jesus before His Jordan baptism."[5]

At His baptism, the Holy Spirit descended upon Jesus (Matthew 3:16). Only Matthew and Luke record the virgin birth, but all four gospels point out that the Holy Spirit came upon Jesus at

---

[5] Maynard James, *I Believe in the Holy Ghost*, Minneapolis, MN: Bethany Fellowship, 1965, pp. 38-39.

His baptism in a fullness which He had not known before in His flesh (Mark 1:10; Matthew 3:16; Luke 3:22; John 1:33). Jesus did not try to run ahead of God. He waited until He was filled with the power of the Holy Spirit before He began to do the work of the Lord.

What is the parallel truth in the life of the believer? No believer, no matter how consecrated or clean or dedicated, can do the work of God without the power of God (John 15:5; Zech. 4:6; Acts 1:8; 1 Cor. 4:20). He must be filled and empowered by the Holy Spirit before he does this. Warning: If we are not very careful, we will lay our plans. We will work until we are knocked out from exhaustion. Yet we will see little results. Our works will be effective only when we do them in the power of the Holy Spirit.

3. Jesus Christ prevailed over the devil in the power of the Holy Spirit. It is significant that the first place the Holy Spirit led Jesus after His baptism was face to face with the devil. He did not lead Him immediately into His public ministry, for He was not ready until He had defeated the devil. The Holy Spirit thrust Jesus out into the wilderness to battle with Satan (Mark 1:12).

In the wilderness the temptations of Jesus were the temptations which a man faces in the flesh. In other words, they were real. How would Jesus face them? He did not say to Satan, "I am the Son of God, endowed with the power of deity, and you cannot defeat me." He met the devil face to face in the body of the flesh, and Luke makes it clear that He defeated him in the power of the Holy Spirit. "And Jesus being full of the Holy Spirit returned from the Jordan and was led by the Spirit into the wilderness" (Luke 4:1). "And immediately the Spirit driveth Him into the wilderness" (Mark 1:12).

It is interesting that when Jesus quoted Scriptures to the devil, He did not choose a verse that would apply only to the Son of God. Thank God, He chose a Scripture that fits you and me and any other human being. He said to Satan, "It is written, man shall not live by bread alone, but by every Word that proceedeth out of the mouth of God" (Deut.8:3; Matt. 4:4). This was the answer of Jesus to Satan. He makes it clear that He is resisting Satan as a man, in the flesh, through the power of the Word and the Holy Spirit.

What is the parallel truth in the life of God's people? It is simply this: No matter how strong you are in your own personality, no matter how informed you may be, you can stand against Satan only in the power of the Holy Spirit. The devil is too much for our person, our knowledge, our dedication.

Believe me when I tell you that one of the finest young women in our church once sat before me (she had held the highest offices a woman can hold in the church) and confessed the most sordid sins. When I asked her how she fell into such, she admitted that she had tried to fight Satan in her own understanding, accomplishments, and power, but he overcame her.

No person is a match for Satan. Jesus, the God man, shows this to us. And today Satan is devouring thousands of good people, and they have not the defense to defeat him.

Life is a wilderness. It is absolutely filled with defeat and bewilderment. Many good people have lost their way. They are spinning their wheels in the wilderness. Or they are sitting under the Juniper tree. They are lost to God, the church, and themselves. The only way out of the wilderness is through the power of the

Holy Spirit. The Living Lord does not intend His people to stay in the wilderness. He has promised deliverance, provided we will appropriate the power of the Holy Spirit.

4. Jesus Christ did His mighty works in the power of the Holy Spirit. Note again Acts 10:38; Luke 4:18; Acts 1:8, 4:31.

5. Jesus performed His miracles in the power of the Holy Spirit. Do you read of any miracles before his baptism? No. In Matthew 12:28 Jesus says, "If I cast out devils by the Spirit of God then the Kingdom of God is come upon you." In Luke 11:20, He says, "If I with the finger of God cast out devils, then no doubt the Kingdom of God is come upon you." The point is that the Spirit of God and finger of God are the same with Jesus. The finger of God is the means through which God accomplishes His purposes on earth (Ex. 31:18; Deut. 9:10; Ex. 8:19; Psalm 8:3). The "finger" with Jesus was none other than the Holy Spirit.

6. Jesus preached and He taught in the power of the Holy Spirit. In His first sermon, He began by saying,

The Spirit of the Lord is upon Me because He has anointed Me to preach the gospel to the poor; He hath sent Me to heal the broken hearted; to preach deliverance to the captives, and recovering of sight to the blind, to set at liberty them that are bruised.

Luke 4:18

I do not understand it. But here it is stated that the Son of God was anointed to preach and teach. Why? I do not understand fully. But I know it is to show you and me that we cannot preach and teach without the anointing.

After Jesus had preached on that first day, Luke 4:22 gives the reaction:

And all bore Him witness and wondered at the gracious words which proceeded out of His mouth. And they said, 'Is not this Joseph's son?'…And they were astonished at His doctrine; for His word was with power" 4:32

What is the parallel in Christian experience today? If we preach and teach without the presence of the Holy Spirit's power, we are leaving the impression that the gospel is without power. We leave the impression that Jesus is really not able to save, that He is really not alive. We also give people the impression that Christianity is the mere activities of man, rather than the supernatural work of God in the heart. I fear we have produced many Pharisees who know a little doctrine, but who know not the power of Jesus in their living (2 Tim. 3:5; 1 Cor. 4:20).

7. Jesus showed the close connection between Himself and the Holy Spirit in His teaching on the blasphemy of the Spirit. Through the power of the Holy Spirit Jesus cast out devils, and His enemies charged, "This fellow doth not cast out devils, but by Beelzebub, the prince of the devils" (Matthew 12:24). The Pharisees were charging that Jesus did His miracles through Satan's power. You will note that the Pharisees said nothing about the Holy Spirit. They criticized Jesus and what He was doing. But the Holy Spirit working in Jesus wrought these miracles. To criticize the actions of Jesus was to criticize the Holy Spirit. To say that these miracles, wrought by the Spirit, were done in the power of Beelzebub, was to

blaspheme the Holy Spirit, a sin with no forgiveness now and forever (Mark 3:28-29).

II. The Indispensable Role of the Holy Spirit In Christian Theology

1. The Holy Scriptures were written by man, but only as they were "moved upon" by the Holy Spirit who superintended the writing of each word, making sure that it was the "God breathed" Word of God (2 Timothy 3:16-17; 2 Peter 1:20-21).

2. Sacrifice – Jesus purchased our redemption in His death, burial and resurrection (1 Cor. 15:3-4) and then ascended back to heaven, whereupon His first act was to send forth the "promise of the Holy Spirit" to the church (Acts 2:33) who revealed Jesus personally to human kind (John 16:7-11) and without which the Holy Spirit would be the "great unknown" in the human heart to quote the great preacher, James Stewart. However, Jesus "offered Himself to God without spot through the Eternal Spirit" (Heb. 9:14).

3. Salvation is experienced when the Holy Spirit enters into one's life through the new birth. But without the gift of the Holy Spirit, there would never have been a new birth and never any experience of salvation (John 3:3,5; 1 Cor. 12:3).

4. Sanctification is the ongoing work of the Holy Spirit following the new birth, wherein one is not only set apart to serve the Lord but also made partakers of the "divine nature." No man could attain unto holiness of life without the sanctifying power of the Holy Spirit (1 Peter 1:2).

5. Spiritual gifts are not mere natural talents, but they are miraculous gifts bestowed upon every believer, whereby he is enabled to serve the Lord and his brothers in the church and the world. These are the "gifts" of the Holy Spirit while the new birth is the Gift, and without the Holy Spirit (Acts 2:38) there would be no gifts whereby the redeemed could acceptably serve the Lord (1 Cor. 15:7ff; 1 Peter 4:10).

6. Spiritual fruit is produced only by the Holy Spirit. The Greeks emphasized what they called the "Cardinal Virtues," (justice, prudence and fortitude) but they were not the same as the fruit of the Holy Spirit; for the fruit of the Holy Spirit is nothing less than the character of Jesus Himself reproduced in the believer by the Holy Spirit, and without Him, they could never be (Gal. 5:22-23).

7. Supplication, to be effective, must also have both the motivation and intercession of the Holy Spirit. Even the apostle Paul did not know how he should pray as he ought, and depended upon the intercession of the Holy Spirit to get through to his Father. So must we, as declared in Romans 8:26; Ephesians 6:18; Jude 1:20.

8. Stewardship – The Jews gave 23 ½ percent of all they possessed prior to the coming of the Holy Spirit, but after He came "All the believers were together and had everything in common. Selling their possessions and goods, they gave to anyone as he had need." (Acts 2:44-45). Before the Spirit changes one's values, he tends to give out of necessity but not out of the heart; after the Holy Spirit comes, people give out of the heart unto

the Lord and others, beginning with the tithe and continuing beyond as "the Lord has prospered them" (1 Cor. 16:2; 2 Cor. 9: 6-8).

9. Soul-Winning – So indispensable is the Holy Spirit for effective witness and soul-winning, that Jesus ordered the apostles not to "depart from Jerusalem until they were endued (clothed) with power (of the Holy Spirit) from on high (Luke 24:49). They obeyed Him and "went preaching (gossiping) the gospel everywhere (Acts 8:4) and "great grace" was upon everyone (Acts 4:33). Such would be impossible without the Holy Spirit (Acts 1:8).

10. Service apart from the power of the Holy Spirit is powerless and ineffective. "Not by the might of man or the power of man, but by My Spirit, saith the Lord of hosts" (Zech. 4:6).

11. The Strength of mankind is not sufficient to live the Christian life and to serve the Lord effectively: Such strength is supplied by the Holy Spirit, so Paul testifies, "I can do all things through the power of Christ which flows out of me." (Phil.

4:13). But without Him, the Holy Spirit, one can do NOTHING (John 15:5).

12. The Body (<u>Soma</u>) of Christ, the church. Before the coming of the Holy Spirit, God's people gathered in assemblies in the wilderness, called the <u>Kahal</u>, but there never was the miracle of the church until the Day of Pentecost. Why? On that day the Holy Spirit came and created the body of Christ through the baptism of the Holy Spirit and the bestowal of spiritual fruit and the spiritual gifts upon all the people of God. What a marvelous creation – what an unprecedented reality for the people of God of all denominations – Baptomethopaliancongrepresbygationalists. St. Augustine declared that Pentecost was the <u>Dies Natalis</u> (birthday of the church). So it was but never would have been had the Holy Spirit not come (1 Cor. 12:13).

III. The Indispensable Role of the Holy Spirit In Christian Experience

The apostle Paul encountered 12 persons in Ephesus who professed they were saved but were resting on a false profession. Significantly, Paul did not ask them if they believed in Christ or had been baptized, or joined a church, but "Did you receive the Holy Spirit when you believed?" Whereupon they replied, "We have not so much as heard whether they be any Holy Spirit" (Acts 19:2-3). Realizing they were not truly saved, Paul shared the gospel, they then trusted Christ, received the Holy Spirit and were truly saved. The person who does not know the Holy Spirit of God does not know God. It's that simple. It's true that God so loved the world that He gave His only begotten Son to provide eternal salvation and that, through His death and resurrection, we have victory over sin and new life in Christ. But apart from the Holy Spirit, God's great salvation is of no relevance to us. Apart from the active work of the Spirit in our lives, we would neither know God nor have the ability to respond to Him. Divine truth is not something we "discover;" it is revealed by the Holy Spirit of God. As such, no other reality in the Christian life is as important as being filled with the Spirit.

The doctrine of the Holy Spirit is distinctive to the Christian faith. No other religion has anything like it. What believers in Jesus Christ have come to know and experience through His gift of the Spirit brings them into a relationship with God that's inaccessible in all other religions of the world. For just as God did not create the world and then step back and watch it spin, but chose to enter time and space and interact with His people, so also God did not just deliver a set of laws for us to follow in the hope of earning our way to heaven. Instead He chose to enter a relationship with His people on earth through His indwelling Spirit."[6]

Our personal relationship with the Holy Spirit – our salvation, our position, and spiritual condition – may be summarized by five wonderful accomplishments of the Holy Spirit in the believer's life:

1. The New Birth of the Holy Spirit. The New Birth is the entrance of the Holy Spirit into an individual when he truly repents of

[6] Henry Blackaby, *Experiencing the Spirit*, Colorado Springs, Colorado: Multnomah Books, 2009, p. 11-12.

his sins, and trusts Jesus as Lord and Savior. This experience is necessary for entrance into the kingdom of God on this earth and the eternal kingdom in the world to come. No one is exempt from needing this experience. To the "Biggest Cog" in the synagogue, Nicodemus, "the teacher of Israel" (John 3:10), Jesus pressed home to his heart "You must be born again" (John 3:3, 3:5, 3:7).

2. The Baptism of the Holy Spirit. This is the gracious act by which an individual, at the time of the new birth, is baptized or placed into the body of Christ. "By one Spirit we were all baptized (past tense) into one body...and have been made to drink into one Spirit" (1 Cor. 12:13). This is a one time experience, unrepeatable, and irrevocable. Some have confused the baptism and the infilling of the Holy Spirit, but they are two different acts according to the Scripture. Never in Scripture are we commanded to be baptized by the Holy Spirit, since our baptism by the Spirit occurred when we were born again. On the other hand, we are commanded to be "continually filled" with the Holy Spirit (Ephesians 5:18). The baptism is our fixed position; the infilling is our conditional spiritual condition.

3. The Indwelling of the Holy Spirit. The Holy Spirit enters into all true believers when they are truly born again. He does not enter into our lives on a temporary camping trip, but He comes to dwell in us forever. Under the Old Covenant, the Holy Spirit could be withdrawn, but Jesus assured His first followers that He would "abide with them forever" (John 14:16). This is the crucial difference that Pentecost made, namely, the Holy Spirit became the permanent gift of God's people and the church "unto the day of redemption" (Ephesians 4:30).

4. The Filling of the Holy Spirit. "The filling represents our spiritual condition in Christ."[7] Being filled means more than being indwelt by Him. It is possible for the Holy Spirit to be present in the life without being president; or to put it another way, one may have the Holy Spirit (His indwelling) but the Holy Spirit may not have him. The filling occurs when one surrenders all to Jesus Christ and makes Him Lord of all.

5. The Anointing of the Holy Spirit. This represents our spiritual vocation. Jesus Himself, though filled with the Holy Spirit, did

---

[7] Stephen F. Olford, *Anointed Expository Preaching*, Broadman Publishing: Nashville, Tennessee, 1998, p.216.

no ministry until after His anointing by the Holy Spirit at His baptism (Acts 10:38). If Jesus saved no souls, healed no sick bodies, performed no miracle until after His anointing, how dare we seek to minister without the anointing. "The filling of the Holy Spirit suggests an 'inward working of the Spirit,' the anointing stresses the outward power for service."[8]

The secret of experiencing the New Birth is simply repentance (turning from sin), asking and receiving God's forgiveness, and trusting Jesus (surrendering) as Lord and Savior. The indwelling and anointing of the Holy Spirit determine our spiritual condition and the effectiveness of our ministry. Thus we need to understand how to be filled and also the secret to the anointing, which will be explained in the final and climatic chapter of this book.

---

[8] Ibid. p. 217.

IV. The Indispensable Role of the Holy Spirit
In Evangelism and Missions

There can be no true evangelism or mission apart from the Holy Spirit. Jesus commanded His first followers to "Go into all the world and make disciples of all the nations" (Matthew 28:19). However, He told them not to go until they had been "endued with power from on high" (Luke 24:49).

> Tarry ye in the city of Jerusalem" until power came upon them, He commanded. His final words, just prior to His ascension, was the assurance that they would soon receive power, after which they would witness to the ends of the earth. "But ye shall receive power, after the Holy Spirit is come upon you and you shall be witnesses unto Me both in Jerusalem, and in all Judea, and in Samaria and unto the uttermost parts of the earth"
> Acts 1:8

These first Christians obeyed Jesus. They "tarried in Jerusalem" until the Day of Pentecost, were all filled with the Holy Spirit (Acts 2:4), they (the lay persons) "went everywhere preaching (gossiping) the gospel" (Acts 8:4). Just a short time later they had won the distinction of being the people "who turned the world upside down" (Acts 17:6). By AD 313 Christianity had become such a powerful force in the Roman Empire that the Roman Emperor, Constantine, fought under the banner of the cross and made Christianity legal throughout the Empire. The late Dr. James Kennedy averred that if Christians had continued to witness in the power of the Holy Spirit as they did for the first 300 years, the whole world would have been evangelized by AD 500. What happened? Clericalism crept into the church with the teaching that only clergy could win the lost. So the church was corrupted by an error still with us, "Let Clerical George do it."

What a tragedy. Suppose the USA is at war, and our "Commander-in-chief," our President, says to our nation, "Wars are dangerous and hard, and ordinary citizens should not be expected to fight, so we are only going to send the Generals to fight our battles." Would we ever win a war with a handful of Generals, who "Generally" do not fight in the first place. Of course not, but that is what the church of Jesus Christ has done in the main until today only five out of 100 professing Christians ever seek to win anybody to Christ.

However, if we are to evangelize at home or abroad (missions) we can do so only in the power of the Holy Spirit. The early Christians waited for Pentecost, for the Holy Spirit could not come until Jesus died and was resurrected and glorified (John 7:39). Thus it must be noted that the early Christians were waiting for Pentecost. Christians today do not need to wait for Pentecost. The Holy Spirit has already come. He has entered into His new temple, our physical bodies. Thus while the early Christians waited for Pentecost and the Holy Spirit, Pentecost is waiting for us today – first to be born of Him, to be baptized into Christ's body, to be indwelt, to be filled, and to be walking in His power, enabling us to witness and to win to the ends of the earth.

In our time there has been a refreshing resurgence of emphasis on the infallibility of the Holy Scriptures. In the SBC, we call this historic event, "The Conservative Resurgence," meaning a return to the Bible as absolute, and infallible authority. Still we have not, at the same time, witnessed a resurgence of evangelism and missions.

What we desperately need now is "The Conservative Resurgence of the Recovery of the Indispensable Role of the Holy Spirit in Evangelism and Missions."

V. The Indispensable Role of the Holy Spirit
In the Advancement of the Church

The advance of the church through the ages has been directly proportional to its experiencing the power of the Holy Spirit. The Book of Acts is a clear and powerful witness of this truth. Beginning with a membership of 120 persons, the early church exploded into phenomenal growth and conquest. It is estimated by some scholars that the church at Pentecost reached a membership of as many as 50,000 to 100,000 in a short period of time. The history of the early church is the Book of Acts, but was named by man, not God, for the name implies that the book records the "Acts" of the apostles and early Christians, when in fact the Book of Acts tells the exciting story of the "Acts of the Holy Spirit" through the Apostles and early Christians. The first missionaries were sent out from a church filled and taught by the Holy Spirit – the church at Antioch. The Holy Spirit said to that church, "Separate me Barnabas and Saul for the work whereunto I have called them…" So they being sent forth by the Holy Spirit departed…" (Acts 13-14). These missionaries later returned and gave a report of their missions to the church. Listen to the description of their report: "And when they were come, and had gathered the church together, they rehearsed ALL THAT GOD had done with them and how He had opened the door of faith unto the Gentiles" (Acts 14:27). Note carefully to whom they gave credit for their work, not themselves, but "All that God (the Holy Spirit) had done with them."

Throughout the ages, when the church has risen to its highest level of power and effectiveness, it has come through a renewed emphasis on the Holy Spirit. The Reformation brought forth a revival in the preaching of the pure Word of God. The creeds or confessions of all Christian bodies were basically orthodox. However, by the 18th century the church had lost its passion, its heart, and with it, evangelism and missions. Then God raised up John Wesley, who being born again and filled with the Holy Spirit, began to preach, "Ye must be born again," and Scriptural holiness, as the way of the Christian life. A mighty revival resulted in England, and according to the historian, Lecky, saved England from a devastating revolution like the French across the channel were experiencing.

At the same time the Great Awakening was taking place in America under the powerful preaching of Jonathan Edwards,

George Whitfield, the Tennent Brothers, and others. Dr. Vernon Standfield proved, in his doctoral thesis, that the Great Awakening (1725-1780) prepared the American colonies to fight the Revolutionary War.[9]

During this same century, when Baptists were doctrinally sound but spiritually anemic, God raised up a man by the name of Shubal Stearns. Stearns was converted under the Spirit-filled preaching of George Whitfield in Connecticut. Finding no haven in the North or even in Virginia, Shubal came to Sandy Creek, North Carolina, located in Randolph County, in central North Carolina, and fathered one of the greatest revivals in history. He was a Separatist Baptist, and his chief emphasis was on the "Indispensable Role of the Holy Spirit" in the Christian life and evangelism and missions. In a word, the Separatist Baptists realized that the work of God is not "By might or power (of man) but by the Holy Spirit, thus saith the Lord" (Zech. 4:6). It must be stated that Shubal Stearns joined the Word and the Spirit, for he understood that God works through two instruments: His Word and Spirit.

---

[9] Thesis in Library of SBTS, Louisville, Kentucky

VI. The Holy Spirit is Indispensable In Prophecy

The Presence of the Holy Spirit indwelling the church and every believer is the "restraining" power against evil in the world "until He is taken out of the way," that is, in the Rapture (2 Thess. 2:7). After His removal, evil will go unrestrained and will reign throughout the world, making it the time of the "Great Tribulation" (Rev. 7:14), a season of unprecedented trouble according to Jesus Himself (Matthew 24:21). The Holy Spirit will leave the world as the abiding indweller of the church and each Christian. However, the Holy Spirit is eternal, omnipresent and sovereign and will still be in the world, convicting people of sin and to saving faith in Jesus Christ. Thus His removal does not mean no one will be saved during the Tribulation. One hundred forty four thousand Jews, 12,000 from each tribe of Israel, will be sealed by the Holy Spirit" during this time, followed by a "multitude which no man could number, of all nations, and people and kindreds and tongues…" (Rev. 7:9). Those being saved will not be those who have heard the gospel previously, but those who hear it for the first time (2 Thess.

45

2:10-12). During these days two witnesses shall be dispatched from heaven to earth who will be given "power" to prophesy one thousand two hundred and sixty days (Rev. 11:3). After this period the Anti-Christ will kill them, but three days later the Holy Spirit will enter into their bodies, raise them from the dead and they will ascend back into heaven (Revelation 11:3-12).

VII. The Holy Spirit is Indispensable In the Rebirth of Israel

In Ezekiel 37, the prophet pictures the nations of Israel and Judah as dead, a veritable "valley of dry bones." He was ordered to prophesy to the bones that they would come to life. The first time he spoke the Word of God, the "sinews, flesh...and ...skin came upon the bones." The next time he prophesies to the wind or breath, the Holy Spirit and breath came into the bodies. This pictured the national restoration and rebirth of Israel (Exek. 37:11-14), first the restoration of a people spiritually dead, and then their regeneration. Thus the Holy Spirit will be indispensable in the rebirth of Israel, promised by God in the Old Testament. We should notice the precise parallel in our own regeneration. There must first be the Word of the Lord (verse 4) but also the Spirit (breath) of life (verse 9), without which there could be no new birth.

Dr. Kyle Yates makes an application to our own need of the breath of life today in our individual lives and churches:

With weirdness, realism and dramatic force the prophet presents the heartening news that Israel may hope to live. A revival is possible! Even dry bones, without sinew and flesh and blood, can live. The coming of God's Spirit brings life. The same thrilling truth is still needed in a world that has dry bones everywhere (not just the world, but the church at large). What we need is to have the Holy Spirit come with His quickening power that a genuine revival may sweep the earth.[10]

---

[10] Quoted in William McDonald, *Believer's Commentary*, p. 1063.

VIII. The Indispensable Role of the Holy Spirit In the Revelation of Jesus

The blasphemy of the Holy Spirit is the only unpardonable sin or a sin which has no forgiveness according to Jesus (Mark 3:29), neither in this world or the world to come (Matt. 12:32). Moreover, Jesus went on to say, "Whosoever speaks a word against the Son of Man, it shall be forgiven him." Does this mean that the Holy Spirit is more important in God's redemptive plan than Jesus Christ? Absolutely not. However, the work of the Holy Spirit and Jesus is different. The work of Jesus is Redemption, and He has finished it and is now seated at the right hand of the Father in heaven. The work of the Holy Spirit is to reveal the redeeming work of Jesus and make it real in all those who trust Jesus as Savior and Lord. For one to blaspheme (regard with contempt and speak against) the Holy Spirit, therefore, is to refuse the only revelation of Jesus Christ human beings have on this earth, thus sealing his doom forever. The seriousness of the blasphemy of the Holy Spirit shows above all the indispensable role of the Holy Spirit in human redemption, namely, that there can be no redemption without the function of the Holy Spirit.

IX. The Indispensable Role of the Holy Spirit In Persevering in the Faith (Staying in the Battle)

The primary characteristic of the Holy Spirit is holiness – He is the Holy Spirit. Therefore, wherever He fills, His presence creates a hunger for holiness.[11] We are not saved by keeping the commandments, but neither are we immune from obeying the moral law set forth in them. The law of Moses does not enable us to keep the law, but the Holy Spirit accomplishes this wonder. Paul asserts this glorious truth in Romans 8:3-4,

> For what the law could not do, God did by sending His own Son in the likeness of sinful flesh and for sin condemned sin in the flesh in order that the righteous requirement (<u>diakoma</u>) might be fulfilled in us who walk not after the flesh but after the Spirit.

---

[11] Donald Whitney, *Spiritual Disciplines of the Christian Life,* p. 237.

Furthermore, Paul is bold to write these words in Gal. 5:16, "Walk ye in the Spirit and you will never under any circumstances (ou me) fulfill the lusts of the flesh." Of course, any discipline of our rebellious flesh is difficult (Heb. 12:11), but the Holy Spirit produces within the yielded believer the power to discipline himself. In fact, He gives the gift of a disciplined mind (2 Tim. 1:7) – sophronismou. The primary office of the Holy Spirit is to glorify Christ, and He does so preeminently by making believers "conform to the image of Christ" (Romans 8:29).

There are days when you are tempted to give up on being a Christian, or you become totally disgusted with the people of God, and are tempted to abandon the spiritual disciplines, but you still "hang in there."[12] Why? It is the Holy Spirit who is causing you to persevere. Dr. W. A. Criswell, the gallant pastor of the largest Baptist church in the world for 65 years, when asked how he had survived, even thrived so long, said these words, "My dear lad I would have given up long ago, perhaps even died, had I not snuggled up to Jesus in the power of the Holy Spirit." As a pastor I would have given up long ago, except for the blessed Holy Spirit who would revive my spirits, even quicken my mortal body (Romans 8:11). Often

---

[12] Ibid. p. 238

before I go to the pulpit to preach, I feel I can't make it, but I lie down on the couch in my study, look up to heaven and quote Phil. 4:13, "I can do all things through the power of Christ which flows in me," and I arise on the wings of an eagle.

Many times I have sung the little song,

> Why should I feel discouraged, why should the shadows come,
> Why should my heart be lonely, and long for heav'n and home,
> When Jesus is my portion? My constant Friend is He:
> His eye is on the sparrow, and I know He watches me;
> His eye is on the sparrow, and I know He watches me.

> Refrain:
> I sing because I'm happy, I sing because I'm free,
> For His eye is on the sparrow, and I know He watches me."

Then the Holy Spirit revives my soul again.

X. The Indispensable Role of the Holy Spirit In the Matter of Prayer

In the area of prayer, the Holy Spirit is the great and constant prompter. How wonderful have been the times all through the night and day when the Holy Spirit would call me to prayer. Dr. R. G. Lee expressed to me his experience in words like this, "I have at times felt a blanket of love cover me through the night." I have felt the same and would to the Holy Spirit that I might experience the same more often. Someone has said, "The only predictable thing about the Holy Spirit is His unpredictability." Not true. While there is great mystery in the work of the Holy Spirit, one thing is certain: He is called alongside of us. That is the very name Jesus gives Him – the Parakeletos – the One like Himself, called alongside of us (John 14:16) to be the Helper we need, and there is no area we need more help than to stay in the battle till He comes, and He is that faithful One to do just that.

Even Paul was imperfect in his praying, so he writes in the first person, "Likewise, the Holy Spirit helps our weaknesses, for we (first person) know not how to pray as we ought, but the Holy Spirit Himself maketh intercession for us with groanings which cannot be uttered" (Romans 8:26). We pray ignorantly, selfishly, narrowly, making it impossible for God to answer. Thus the Holy Spirit "helpeth" us. The word "helpeth" is a 10 letter Greek word, lambenetai, meaning to "take hold of." The picture is of one standing opposite another taking hold with him to lift a load too heavy for him to bear alone. My father used to say to me on the farm as he tried to move a heavy object, "Son, grab a holt." It is just what the Holy Spirit offers to do for us with our burden of prayer. We can be sure also that He will be carrying the heavy end of the burden as we make our way to the throne of grace. How often I have almost despaired in lifting my prayers to God only to depend on the Holy Spirit who brought great comfort to my soul.

XI. The Indispensable Role of the Holy Spirit In Comforting the Soul

Jesus referred to the Holy Spirit as the "One like Himself" who would be called along our side to bring various kinds of comfort. (the Parakletos – John 14:16). The King James translation even translates this word "Comforter," based upon the Latin word Comfortare, meaning, to bring comfort by giving us the needed strength to confront the hard chores of this life. There are various levels of His comfort.

a. One of the greatest comforts He brings is the assurance of our sonship. "The Spirit Himself bears witness with our spirits that we are the sons of God" (Romans 8:14).

b. Another precious comfort is an "Abba Father" relationship with our heavenly Father. "We have not received the spirit of bondage but the spirit of sonship (adoption) whereby we cry Abba Father" (Romans 8:15). "Abba" means "Daddy," or "Papa." Such intimacy is made possible only by the Holy Spirit.

c. A third comfort of the Holy Spirit is His revelation to us that we are "heirs of God and joint heirs of Jesus Christ" (Gal. 4:6-7). Such a revelation does not come through our five senses, but is "revealed to us by the Spirit" (1 Cor. 2:9-10). Heaven itself, though future, is as sure as the rising sun.

"A tent or a cottage, why should I care?
They're building a palace for me over there.
Though exiled from home, yet still I may sing:
All glory to God, I am a child of the King."

Hattie E. Buell

d. Perhaps the very highest form of comfort comes in times of enormous suffering and affliction. At times the Holy Spirit applies the healing virtue of Jesus; but even more often He assures us that God has a redemptive purpose in our suffering and that He is "causing all things to work together for good for those who love the Lord, and are called according to His purpose" (Romans 8:28).

Two women patients in the hospital were overheard discussing their respective physicians. One lady was perturbed because her doctor would not explain what was going on in her body. The other lady felt the opposite and said, "I like my doctor just fine. He takes time to explain what is going on and what he is trying to do. That makes the pain easier to bear." Then she added, "I can stand anything if I know it is helping me get well." The Holy Spirit is like that doctor. If we listen to Him, He will explain, if not all, at least enough of the treatment to help us bear the pain, fully assured that God knows what He is about.[13]

e. The comfort which the Holy Spirit brings may not be a miraculous intervention but simply the constant awareness of God's presence. "I will not leave you orphans, I will come to you" (the Person of the Holy Spirit – John 14:18). "I will never, never, never leave you nor forsake you" (Heb. 13:5). Herein lies the ultimate remedy of human grief and

---

[13] Ralph Herring, *God My Helper*, p. 61.

pain – knowing that God is with you. It is the tendency of sin and sickness to make us feel alone and often that God has forsaken us. Not true. In Psalm 23 David speaks of God in the third person in the first three verses, but in verse four he shifts to the second person and speaks directly to God in these words, "Even though I walk through the shadow of death, I will fear no evil." Why? "For thou art with me." Illus: I was making my way to visit a lady facing surgery when the surgeon caught me in the hall and said, "Dr. Bennett, I hope you can calm Mrs. O'Neal down, for I cannot do surgery until she quietens down. She has raved all night long." I went into the room, stood at Mrs. O'Neal's bedside and asked her this question, "Margaret, do you believe the Bible is God talking to us?" "Yes, indeed." Do you believe it is Jesus speaking to you? "Absolutely." Then please listen to these words as I speak them to you. I then quoted these words:

Fear not, for I am with you; Be not dismayed, for I am your God. I will strengthen you, Yes, I will help you, I will uphold you with My righteous right hand.' For I, the LORD your God, will hold your right hand, Saying to you, 'Fear not, I will help you" (Isaiah 41:10, 13).

The assurance of the presence of Jesus or the Holy Spirit brought an immediate calm to Mrs. O'Neal. I stepped outside and said, "Dr. White, Mrs. O'Neal is now ready for he surgery" and so she was and underwent successful surgery with no problems. Illus: A little girl woke up her father screaming one night. He rushed to her bed to discover she was having a nightmare. Her father calmed her down and assured her that there was nothing to fear, for God was with her. The little girl replied, "I know that, but I need a God with skin on Him." Indeed, we have that God who came to this earth (John 14:17), and then sent the Holy Spirit to be a Comforter like Himself (John 14:16) and no person, no possession, no place, no pleasure can substitute for the Indispensable ministry or role of the Holy Spirit. So we shout with joy the Doxology, "Praise God from whom all blessings flow, praise Him all creatures here below. Praise Father, Praise Son and Holy Ghost."

XII. The Holy Spirit is Indispensable In our Fulfilling the "Righteous Requirements of the Law" (Romans 8:4)

The righteous requirements of the law are to love the Lord Jesus with all our being and our neighbors as ourselves (Matt. 22:37-39). The ceremonial aspect of the Mosaic law has been set aside (Col. 2:14-17), and the civic aspects, which shows the application of the moral law in a community, has been transferred to human government (Romans 13:1-17). The moral law, however remains, is reflected in the character of God, is outlined in the Ten Commandments, and is condensed by Jesus in the Great Commandment: "Thou shall love the Lord thy God with all thy heart, soul and mind, and thou shalt love thy neighbor as thyself" (Matthew 22:37-39).

Although the believer is no longer in bondage to the moral law's condemnation, the law still reflects the moral character of God and is the standard of behavior for all Christ followers. But what the external, written code was unable to accomplish under the Old Covenant, and before the coming of the Holy Spirit at Pentecost, the Holy Spirit is able to do by writing it on our hearts under the New Covenant (Jer. 31:33-34) and giving us the power to obey it who "walk not according to the flesh (our old Adamic nature) but the Spirit" (Romans 8:4b).

To "walk according to the Spirit" is not an admonition but a statement of fact that applies to every true believer. "Walk" refers to lifestyle, the habits of thinking and living that characterize the lives of the truly born again of the Holy Spirit. Since every true Christian is indwelt by the Holy Spirit (Romans 8:9b), every Christian will manifest His fruit, the first of which is Agape love and "love is the fulfillment of the law" (Romans 13:10b). But carefully note that "the righteousness of the law is fulfilled in us," not by us, but by the wonderful power of the indwelling Holy Spirit (Romans 8:4b and Romans 5:5). So you can easily see how utterly indispensable the Holy Spirit is in our obeying the moral law of God. And those who profess they know a holy God but "deny Him" by their lifestyles are "abominable, disobedient...reprobates" (Titus 1:16).

XIII. The Indispensable Role of the Holy Spirit In Worship

In my judgment the most perspicacious word on worship in the Bible is found in Phil. 3:3 when Paul writes these insightful words, "We are the true circumcision, who worship in the Spirit (Holy) of God and glory in Jesus Christ and put no confidence in the flesh." These words are a succinct identification of true worship of those who truly worship, namely, those who have experienced true circumcision, which is the birth of the Spirit (Deut. 30:6), and also the purpose of worship – "to glorify Jesus Christ" and the impossibility of true worship – to worship in our flesh or natural condition. In a word, all true worship is experienced only by those whose hearts have been created anew by the Holy Spirit, whose uttermost motive is to glorify Jesus Christ, and whose hearts are not centered on self (the flesh) but on Holy God alone." Jesus is seeking followers who will worship this way. "God is a Spirit, and those who worship Him must worship Him in spirit and in truth for the Father is seeking such to worship Him" (John 4:24).

And He is seeking them through the Holy Spirit Who is both the prompter and producer of true worship and without Him worship is but a fleshly expression to honor self, not our Savior.

XIV. The Indispensable Role of the Holy Spirit In Understanding the Word of God

In order to understand the true and spiritual meaning of the Word, one must know the author of the Word – the Holy Spirit. Paul makes this utterly clear in his word to the learned Corinthians.

But as it is written:

Eye has not seen, nor ear heard,

Nor have entered into the heart of man

The things which God has prepared for those

who love Him.

But God has revealed them to us through His Spirit. For the Spirit searches all things, yes, the deep things of God. For what man knows the things of a man except the spirit of the man which is in him? Even so no one knows the things of God except the Spirit of God. Now we have received, not the spirit of the world, but the Spirit who is from God, that we might know the things that have been freely given to us by God. These things we also speak, not in words which man's wisdom teaches but which the Holy Spirit teaches, comparing spiritual things with spiritual. But the natural man does not receive the things of the Spirit of God, for they are foolishness to him; nor can he know them, because they are spiritually discerned. 1 Cor. 2:9-14

Of course, if one is a good reader, knowledgeable in grammar and trained in the original languages of Hebrew and Greek, he can interpret the "letter" of the Bible, but he cannot grasp its spiritual content without the Holy Spirit. Such interpretation does not minister life but death. The apostle Paul warned against such a deception when he wrote 1 Cor. 3:5-6.

Ye are manifestly declared to be the epistle of Christ ministered by us, written not with ink, but with the Spirit of the living God; not in tables of stone, but in fleshly tables of the heart…We are not sufficient of ourselves to think anything as of ourselves, but

our sufficiency is of God, who has made us able
ministers of the New Testament, not of the letter
but of the spirit; for the letter killeth, but the spirit
giveth life.

Jesus promised that the soon-coming Holy Spirit (before His
ascension into heaven) would be our interpreter of truth and not
only our interpreter but our wonderful "Remembrancer" (John
14:26). In fact Jesus assured His disciples that it would be to their
advantage for Him to leave them, so He could send the Holy Spirit
who would teach them truth which they could not "bear now"
(John 16:12). Listen to His amazing promise in John 16:7-15.

"Nevertheless I tell you the truth; It is expedient
for you that I go away: for if I go not away, the
Comforter will not come unto you; but if I depart,
I will send Him unto you.

And when He is come, He will reprove the world
of sin, and of righteousness, and of judgment:

Of sin, because they believe not on Me;

Of righteousness, because I go to My Father, and ye see Me no more;

Of judgment, because the prince of this world is judged. I have yet many things to say unto you, but ye cannot bear them now.

Howbeit when He, the Spirit of truth, is come, He will guide you into all truth: for He shall not speak of Himself; but whatsoever He shall hear, that shall He speak: and He will shew you things to come.

He shall glorify Me: for He shall receive of mine, and shall shew it unto you.

All things that the Father hath are Mine: therefore said I, that he shall take of Mine, and shall shew it unto you.

A little while, and ye shall not see Me: and again, a little while, and ye shall see Me, because I go to the Father.

Then said some of his disciples among themselves, What is this that he saith unto us, A little while, and ye shall not see Me: and again, a little while, and ye shall see Me: and, Because I go to the Father?"

I read that on one occasion there were two men who recited the 23rd Psalm. The first man to recite was trained in elocution and the art of speaking to the fullest extent. The audience stood in awe at his ability and eloquence in reciting the Psalm. The second man was relatively unlearned, but after he recited the great Psalm, there was not a dry eye in the audience. What made the enormous difference? The first speaker knew the Psalm; the second speaker knew the author of the Psalm.

And so it must be with us if we would interpret God's Word and be able to share it in power with others.

XV. The Holy Spirit is Indispensable
In the Preaching and Teaching of the Word of God.

A preacher may have good content in his message, and irresistible logic, and a forceful and loud delivery; but without the accompanying power of the Holy Spirit, the message is just another classroom lecture or informational seminar. John Macarthur observed:

> "They may truly love the Word of God and have a high regard for sound doctrine, but what their dispassionate delivery actually communicates is apathy and indifference. In the end they undermined the very work they believe they are called to advance. The world (and the church) would be better off without such preaching."[14]

The apostle Paul knew that the preaching of the Word and the Holy Spirit are inseparable. "For our gospel came not unto you in

---

[14] Quoted in Alex Montoya, *Preaching with Passion*, p. 7.

word only, but also in power, and in the Holy Ghost..." (1 Thess. 1:5). No doubt the apostle was trained in Greek rhetoric and able to speak with "enticing words of man's wisdom," but he did not as he clearly states in 1 Cor. 2:4-5.

The Book of Acts is really a demonstration of the power of God in the preaching and living of the disciples. A brief survey of the church in action leads us to connect its incredible power with the Holy Spirit. Examine these references from the Book of Acts:

Acts 2:4, "And they were all filled with the Holy Spirit and began to speak with other tongues, as the Spirit gave them utterance."

Acts 4:8, "Then Peter, filled with the Holy Spirit, said to them, "Rulers of the people and elders of Israel."

Acts 4:31, "...and they were all filled with the Holy Spirit, and they spoke the word of God with boldness."

Acts 7:55, "But he, being full of the Holy Spirit, gazed into heaven and saw the glory of God, and Jesus standing at the right hand of God,"

Acts 13:9-10, "Then Saul, who also is called Paul, filled with the Holy Spirit, looked intently at him and said, "O full of all deceit and all fraud, you son of the devil, you enemy of all righteousness, will you not cease perverting the straight ways of the Lord?"

Acts 13:52, "And the disciples were filled with joy and with the Holy Spirit."

These were Christians who had a deep personal relationship and reliance upon the Holy Spirit. We need to learn from them for our living and preaching and teaching.

XVI. The Indispensable Role of the Holy Spirit In Crucifying the Flesh.

When any person truly repents and trust Jesus as Lord and Savior, he dies to the old life of sin and self and is risen with Christ "to walk in newness of life" (Romans 6:2-4; 2 Cor. 5:16; 1 John 3:9). In fact that person has died with Christ and risen with Him to live a holy life. All this is pictured in immersion baptism. However, the death which begins to take effect when the believer first accepts Christ must be experienced daily throughout life. This picture clearly presented in baptism is often abandoned, and as a consequence, far too many Christians, confused and discouraged, often abandon the idea of victory over sin and the flesh and live a wretched life torn between the contending forces of flesh and spirit or simply say, "I cannot keep from sinning or living in the flesh."

To make this victory ours is the first work of the Holy Spirit after that of the new birth (regeneration). This aspect of the Holy Spirit's ministry is strikingly set forth in Romans 8:13, "If you live according to the flesh, you will die; but if you by the Spirit put to death the deeds of the body you shall live." The "deeds" of the body are "the doings" of the body, such as "fornication, uncleanness, passion, covetousness, anger, wrath, malice, shameful speaking,...lyin." (Col. 3:5-9). From God's viewpoint, the "deeds of the body" or "old man" (King Self) has been dealt with once and for all – crucified with Christ; but from our viewpoint, the death by crucifixion must be applied to the "doings" of the flesh in a day by day process.

How is the Flesh, King Self, or Deeds of the Body Put to Death? In a word, "The Self Life." Certainly not by the energy of the flesh. I have heard Christians pray, "Lord, help me to crucify myself." No one can crucify himself. It's a physical impossibility. One can commit suicide in many different ways, but if he ever dies by crucifixion someone else will put him on the cross.

The Holy Spirit is the Agent Who Brings Crucifixion to Pass. As Romans 8:13 specifically states, "If ye by the Spirit do put to death the deeds of the body (its doings), ye shall live." In order to understand how the Spirit works with us to put the death sentence into effect, we must understand the meaning of the one word translated "put to death." The word is <u>THANATOS</u>, which means Death. (Note: William Cullen Bryant wrote the famous poem on death called Thanatopsis). To this one word <u>Thanatos</u> is added a causative ending, making it <u>THANAtoute</u>, which literally means "cause to put to death." We are not able to crucify ourselves. However, we are to acknowledge our sin, and give the Holy Spirit permission to crucify it or take it out of our lives. He MUST have our permission. We must say the word, because God does nothing in us without our own active cooperation.

Permit me at this point to share an illustration whereby a pastor friend of mine described how he learned to permit the Holy Spirit to enable him to crucify King Self:

"An experience some years ago brought home to me this aspect of the Holy Spirit's ministry. We had at that time a pet dog named Skipper which had won his way into our affections – especially those of our children. One day Skipper was struck by a passing automobile. Though he recovered in a measure from his injury, Skipper was never himself again. His disposition was ruined and he became a problem in the neighborhood. One day after he had snapped at my little daughter I sent him to the veterinarian for observation. The doctor explained that sometimes a dog's disposition was permanently altered by an injury of that nature. He stated that Skipper would probably be a dangerous pet to have with the little children in the home and frankly advised me to put him down. The veterinarian had made his recommendation. He stood ready to carry out the course that he had advised. But the problem was mine—the dog was mine, and the children were mine. It was my responsibility to say the word, and I said it. I have always felt that I said the right word, and ever since I have held in grateful appreciation the friend who counseled me so wisely and who then so faithfully did the "dirty work" for me. So far as I know that is the only sentence of execution I have pronounced – except that which time and time again I pronounce when the Holy Spirit reveals to me the working of a vicious nature within and waits my word to carry out the death sentence which he so strongly recommends."[15]

---

[15] Ralph Herring, *God Being My Helper,* pp. 25-26

My friend's relation to Skipper describes the position which the believer must take in regard to the problem of the flesh. However the act of pronouncing God's sentence must be cultivated until it becomes habit of mind. That attitude is described in Romans 6:11 where Paul says, "Even so reckon ye also yourselves to be dead unto sin, but alive unto God in Christ Jesus." The tense of the verb is present, indicating a continuing process of reckoning. The word "reckon" means "to accept as an accomplished fact" that our "old man" (Self) has been crucified as the Word plainly states, "Ye died, and your life is hid with Christ in God" (Col. 3:3). "They that are of Christ Jesus have crucified the flesh with the passions and the lusts thereof" (Gal. 5:24). The crucifixion has already taken place. By faith we must accept this fact and hold to the course in a steady reckoning.

Caution: This business of being "dead" to sin does not necessarily take away its appeal, nor does it render us incapable of responding. Many a young believer discovers through painful experience that if sin and self are dead, it is the "livest dead" thing he has ever encountered. The fact is: we are free to do as we choose. God's will is that we play by the rules he has graciously given – quietly reckoning in our minds and faith that we ourselves are dead unto sin and do not have to commit it and alive unto God just as He as said.

> "…The wonderful thing about it is that the instant we make this reckoning and take the position that He has indicated in relation to sin, the whole problem is solved and the victory is won. It is a sure way, and the only way by which the believer may walk in constant victory."[16]

Then the believer will know that Jesus did not just come to give life but to give it more abundantly (John 10:10b).

---

[16] Ibid. p. 27

XVII. The Wonderful Spirit-Filled Life
Ephesians 5:18

God accomplishes His purposes in the believer's life by two instruments: The Word and the Spirit. "All Word and no Spirit, you dry up. All Spirit and no Word, you blow up. Combine the Word and Spirit, you will grow up." The basis of mentoring is the "Internalization of the Word," but the Word without the Holy Spirit will not work the miracle of God's grace in the human heart. We see this very clearly in the experience of the new birth. Jesus commands that we must be born of the Water and the Spirit in order to enter the Kingdom of God (John 3:5). Water speaks of the Word of God (Ephesians 5:26) and the Spirit means the Holy Spirit. It is when the Word of God and the Spirit of God come together in the heart by faith that the miracle of a new life begins.

But the new birth is but the beginning of the work of the Holy Spirit in human experience. When one repents and turns to Jesus as Lord and Savior, the Holy Spirit enters immediately and permanently into that person (1 Cor. 6:19; Romans 8:9b). We call this His indwelling. Simultaneously, the Holy Spirit baptizes the believer into the body of Christ once and for all (1 Cor. 12:13). This is the real baptism of the Holy Spirit. All these divine acts occur at the moment one truly trusts Jesus as Lord and Savior. However, these events do not conclude the work of the Holy Spirit in the believer. Beyond these, God categorically commands through the apostle Paul that every believer be continually filled with the Holy Spirit (Ephesians 5:18). The question naturally arises, why do we need to be filled (controlled) by the Holy Spirit if we already have His indwelling and His baptism. Simply for this reason: You can have the Holy Spirit, but the Holy Spirit may not have you, or to express it another way, the Holy Spirit may be present in you, but He demands to be President in you, that is, to fill or control your life. Let me bring all this truth together under three simple points:

I. The Reasons to be Filled.

There are two main reasons:

(a) God commands it. "Be filled (literally be being filled) with the Holy Spirit" (Ephesians 5:18b). Please notice four facts about this command:

a. First of all, this command is in the imperative mood. This means it is not optional. To be filled is to obey God and reap His blessings; to fail to be filled is to disobey God and miss His blessings.

b. Second, this command is plural in number. This means that this command is given to every believer, not just spiritual giants, pastors, elders or deacons.

c. Third, this command is in the passive voice, which means we cannot fill ourselves but filling comes from an outside source. Our responsibility is to put ourselves in a position where the Spirit of God can control us.

d. Fourth, this command is in the present tense. Unlike the new birth and baptism of the Holy Spirit, which happens only once in a believer's life, the filling of the Holy Spirit is a repeated event. In essence, the text commands, "Be ye being filled with the Holy Spirit." Both Adrian Rogers and James Merritt, noted pastors and preachers, have said, "It is a far greater sin for a child of God not to be filled with the Holy Spirit than for a person to get drunk on alcoholic beverages."

(b) The demands of the Christian life require it. The demands of the Christian life cannot be met by our natural will power, but only by the supernatural power of God released in our lives. Who within his own power can "love his enemies" (Matthew 5:44)? Who in his own power can "rejoice ever more" (1 Thess. 5:16)? Who in his own power can fulfill the righteous requirements of the law (Romans 8:2-4)?

II. The Requirements to be Filled. A great theologian has said, "The good things of the Kingdom of God do not belong to the well meaning but to the desperate." Candidates for the infilling must "mean business" with the Lord. The casual Christian and the average Sunday morning attendee do not qualify.

First, you must have been born of the Holy Spirit before you can be filled.

Secondly, you must desire with all your heart to be filled. Only those who "hunger and thirst...will be filled" (Matthew 5:6).

Thirdly, you must believe that God will fill you, not just can fill you.

Fourthly, you must denounce all known sin in your life. You must do more than confess sin (admit it); you must abandon it (Prov. 28:13).

Fifthly, you must dethrone self and enthrone Christ as Lord of all. This would mean that you would take your control over your life and turn it over to the living Christ.

Sixthly, you must by faith ask the Holy Spirit to fill you (Luke 11:13).

Seventhly, you must accept the fact that He has filled you and live with total dependence on Him saying, "Lord God, I yield control of my life to you today. Just show me what to do." This would mean that you are walking in the Spirit (Gal. 5:16).

In a word, you must surrender your life to Jesus Christ as your Lord. Please notice that I did not say "commit" your life, but to surrender it. When you commit, you determine the things you will commit; when you surrender, the Lord determines the things you will surrender. Commitment would be like taking a plain sheet of paper and writing on that paper the things you would commit to the Lord and then signing your name at the bottom. Surrender would mean something entirely different. You would not write anything on the blank sheet of paper, but you would sign your name at the bottom and ask the Lord Jesus Christ to fill in the top. Be sure not to confuse surrender with the "time honored" re-dedications which take place in many churches with little or no continuing results. Rededications are the very opposite of surrender, as is commitment, and will never result in the filling of the Holy Spirit.

III. The Result of Being Filled:

(a) The person who is filled will overflow with the fruit of the Holy Spirit (Gal. 5:22-23).

(b) The person who is filled will have an intimate (Abba Father) relationship with His Father in heaven (Romans 8:15).

(c) The person who is filled will be a bold witness to the ends of the earth (Acts 1:8).

(d) The person who is filled with the Holy Spirit will have victory over indwelling sin (Romans 8:13).

(e) The person who is filled with the Holy Spirit will be enabled to exercise his gifts in the power of God (John 14:12).

(f) The person who is filled with the Holy Spirit will be powerful in prayer (Acts 4:31).

(g) The person who is filled with the Holy Spirit will have deep understanding of the Bible (1 Cor. 2:9-10).

(h) The person who is filled with the Holy Spirit will worship in "Spirit and in truth" (John 4:24; Ephesians 5:19).

(i) The person who is filled with the Holy Spirit will carry out his duties in his home (Ephesians 5:21; 5:25; 6:1).

In a word, the Spirit-filled person will live the normal Christian life, the one God ordained for him at the time of his new birth (Ephesians 1:3).

D.L. Moody preached without the infilling for years, but one day was filled while walking the streets of New York City; then he made this statement, "You can see without eyes, hear without ears, chew without a tongue, and breath without lungs sooner than you could live the Christian life without the infilling of the Holy Spirit."

Personally, I was a defeated preacher and pastor until the Holy Spirit revealed to me, on the streets of Greensboro, North Carolina, that He was my "<u>Paracletos</u>," (John 14:16) the one who was coming beside me, to give me the power, motivation, perseverance, all I needed to both live for Him and serve Him with great joy. Hallelujah – that was the beginning of a new day in my life, without which I believe I would have despaired long before now.

In closing, I feel impressed to share with you the testimony of the late Adrian Rogers concerning the need for the fullness of the Holy Spirit.

"I want you to imagine a man who has bought, for the first time in his life, a brand-new automobile. He's never driven before, never had an automobile, and what he does not understand is that it has an engine in it.

He is proud of the car. He invites his friends over and shows them how beautiful the paint job is, how soft the seats are. And he says, "See how nice this is, what a sleek automobile this is." But everywhere he goes, he has to push it. Sometimes when he is going downhill, he can get in and coast, but that doesn't excite him to much because he knows every hill that he coasts down he's got to push that thing up the next hill.

While he's proud of his automobile and in some ways grateful that he has it, in other ways he secretly wishes he didn't have it. Rather than being a blessing to him, it became a burden to him. Rather than it carrying him, he has to push it.

And then somebody says, "I want to show you something. See that thing. That's called an ignition key. Put it right in there and turn it. Vroom!" "What's that?" "That's a thing called the engine. Now take that lever right there and put it where it says 'D' and then press that pedal," and that automobile begins to surge forth with power. "Hey," he says, "This is wonderful, this is glorious, this is amazing.

Why didn't somebody tell me before? Why didn't somebody show me this before?"

You say, "That's foolish. Nobody could be that dumb." You're right, unless it is the Christian who does not understand the power of the Holy Spirit of God.

Many Christians don't understand that when they got saved, God put an engine in their salvation. I don't mean to speak disrespectfully about the Holy Spirit by calling Him an engine, but He is the dynamism, the power of our Christian life. Many people are somewhat proud of their Christianity, but it's almost a burden to them. Rather than it carrying them, they are pushing it. And they're just grinding out this matter of being a Christian because they have not made the discovery of the wonderful Spirit-filled life. Ephesians 5:18 has a command of God: "And do not be drunk with wine, in which is dissipation; but be filled with the Spirit."

When you are filled with the Spirit, it will turn the drudgery to dynamism. Rather than making your Christianity a burden, it will become an empowering blessing to you."[17]

---

[17] Adrian Rogers, *What Every Christian Ought To Know*, Nashville Tennessee, Broadman and Holman Publishers, 2005, pp. 168-169.

Biblography

Bennett, Bill. *Thirty Minutes to Raise the Dead*. Nashville: Thomas Nelson Publishers, 1991.

Blackaby, Henry & Melvin, *Experiencing the Spirit*. Colorado Springs: Multomah Books, 2009.

Brooks, Phillips. *The Joy of Preaching*. Grand Rapids: Kregel Publications, 1989.

Chan, Francis. *Forgotten God*. Colorado Springs: David C. Cook, 2009.

Criswell, W. A. *The Holy Spirit in Today's World*. Grand Rapids: Zondervan Publishing House, 1966.

Graham, Billy. *The Holy Spirit.* Nashville: Word Publishing, 1978, 1988.

Hayford, Jack. *Living the Spirit Formed Life.* Ventura: Regal Books, 2001.

Hemphill, Kenneth S. *Spiritual Gifts.* Nashville: Broadman Press, 1988.

Heisler, Greg. *Spirit-Led Preaching.* Nashville: Academic Publishing House, 2007.

Herring, Ralph. *God Being My Helper.* Broadman Press, 1955.

Hession, Roy. *The Calvary Road.* Fort Washington: Christian Literature Crusade, 1950

Horner, Barry E. *Future Israel.* Nashville: Academic Publishing House, 1999.

Kinlaw, Dennis F. *Preaching in the Spirit.* Grand Rapids: Zondervan Publishing House, 1985.

Jeremiah, David. *God In You.* Sisters, Oregon: Multonah, 1998.

Lloyd-Jones, D. Martyn. *Preaching and Preachers: Reviving the Art in the Twentieth Century.* Phillipsburg, N. J.: Presbyterian and Reformed Pub. Co., 1986.

Maynard, James. *I Believe in the Holy Ghost.* Minneapolis: Bethany Fellowship, 1965.

McDill, Wayne. *The Twelve Essential Skills for Great Preaching.* Nashville: Broadman & Holman Publishers, 1994.

Montoya, Alex. *Preaching with Passion.* Grand Rapids: Kregal Publication, 2000.

Morgan, G. Campbell. *Preaching.* Old Tappan, N.J.: Fleming H. Revell, Co., 1937.

Olford, Stephen. *Anointed Expository Preaching.* Nashville: Broadman & Holman Publishers, 1998.

Packer, J.I. *Knowing God.* Downers Grove: Intervarsity Press, 1973.

Pentecost, J. Dwight. *New Wine.* Grand Rapids: Kregel Publication, 2010.

Shaddix, Jim. *The Passion Driven Sermon.* Nashville: Broadman & Holman Publishers, 2003.

Spurgeon, Charles. *What the Holy Spirit Does in a Believer's Life.* Lynwood: Emerald Books, 1993.

Sproul, R. C. *The Mystery of the Holy Spirit.* Lake Mary, Florida: Christian Focus Publication, 2009.

Stanley, Charles F. *Living in the Power of the Holy Spirit.* Nashville: Nelson Books, 2005.

Stanley, Charles F. *The Wonderful Spirit Filled Life*. New York: Walker and Co. 1992.

Swindol, Charles R. *Flying Closer to the Flame*. Dallas: Word Publishing, 1993.

Tozer, A. W. *The Knowledge of the Holy Spirit*. New York: Harper & Brothers, 1961.

Warren, Rick. *God's Power to Change Your Life*. Grand Rapids: Zondervan Publishing House, 1990.

Whitney, Donald. *Spiritual Disciplines of the Christian Life*. Colorado Springs: NavPress, 1991.